BREAKING

THE

BULLYING CIRCLE

ISBN – 978-0-692-75173-2

Table of Table of Contents

Acknowledgements

This book is about my journey from victim to bully to a nationally recognized crusader against bullying. This book will show you many different points of view from the various perspectives of people who have an effect on the continuous escalation of bully-related violence. From parent, to bully, to school official (principal, teacher), to victim, in this book you get to walk in another's shoes, see another side and, maybe, just maybe, you will make amazing changes in yourself. Seeing another's perspective will become a tool that you can add to your Life Skills Toolbox.

The first book in this series, *Building the 21st Century Child*, received great responses as to the ease of the story and how the Toolboxes of Learning encouraged thought in the reader. This book

1

continues the adventure of our teacher/parent Julia and her two children, Zachary and Olivia. As you read through the book, there will be opportunities for you, as the reader, to explore and see the same situation from other perspectives.

Think about when you walk into a clothing store to buy new clothes. Before you make your decision about each individual piece of clothing, you first try it on. Even if, visually, you agree with how the article of clothing looks, you must try it on like it was your own to truly get an understanding of how it feels on you.

That is my challenge to you as an adult who wants the best for the children in your life. You will have your opinions and the inner voice in your head will say, "I don't think like that," or "that doesn't make sense." That is perfect. Your challenge is to **try**

on the conversation or point of view as if it were your own. The Life Skills Toolbox activities will gently guide you. Even after you try it on and it doesn't "fit" at least you were the powerful, responsible adult who tried. That is the first step. Maybe you'll get a better understanding of how another person feels, which could be beneficial in the future. Even if you completely disagree with them, understanding them will help them help you.

I would like to thank every parent and school that I have ever worked with that allowed me to reach more children and open their minds to what is possible. I would like to thank Landmark Education and its staff and volunteers for having amazing workshops that allowed me to open my mind and see what I could do to help others. My first bullying assembly program in 2003 was a project for one of their courses. I would like to thank Jeff Sullivan and the staff at Wisdom Seekers for helping with the logistics of this book and David Levine for his constant support and feedback on this book. Lastly I would like to thank you, the reader, for opening up this book. This won't be your typical read. You may be triggered, confronted and hopefully empowered during different parts of the book. Read as much as you like. Take a break after a chapter. We as humans are slowly and surely drifting away into a living slumber. I invite you to wake up. And I invite you to, when you are done reading this book, give it to someone working in education in hopes that they will choose to wake up as well. I humbly thank you. Enjoy your adventure!

INTRODUCTION

How I Became a Bully

When I was 12 years old, my parents put me in a naval academy military school so that I would become more disciplined and improve my grades. I was a classic underachiever and public schools weren't the best option for me. I was overweight, had Coke bottle glasses, and wore braces. I was the perfect target for bullying, with many different options on how to be bullied.

At five in the morning on my first day, I heard a loud banging on the door. All the new plebes (their version of pledges) had to immediately get to the track for running and drilling exercises. When I got to the track, it was me and the 19 other children (10 to 19 years old) in the platoon. After running about halfway around the track, I couldn't run anymore no matter how hard I tried. I had to stop on the side of the track and throw up. I was told by one of the officers, who were only high school juniors and seniors themselves, that if I didn't keep running, my whole platoon would have to do push-ups because of me. Of course, I wasn't able to continue running because of my lack of previous exercise. I had to stand there at 5:30 in the morning and watch 19 other children do push-ups because I couldn't run. I walked into my room completely distraught, not realizing what I had gotten myself into. I started to get changed and, before I could finish, I felt a hand grab me by the back of my neck. It was an older student, about 16 or 17 years old, who was a lot larger than me. He said, "If I ever have to do push-ups because of you again, I'm going to kill you." That was my first day.

There was absolutely no communication allowed between the children and their parents for the first two weeks. Those two weeks were the longest two weeks of my life. I cried every night and wrote letters to my parents, telling them how much I loved them and how much I missed them. None of those letters ever made it out as my roommate, who was there for beating up his mother, found them and tore them up before I ever had a chance to mail them.

I would be woken up in the middle of the night by my roommate who would go to the bathroom and, on his way back, decide it was a good idea to punch me in my face while I slept. By day three, I was given a nickname by the "officer" who was supposed to be a shining example of leadership. He nicknamed me Gomer Pyle. I did not see the movie *Full Metal Jacket* until 15 years later. Gomer Pyle's character in the movie was bullied (every mistake Pyle made earned punishment for the rest of the platoon, with Pyle being spared) and took his own life. I cried that night, all over again, as I remembered every last detail of what had happened 15 years before.

During those first two weeks, I was repeatedly beaten up. I was thrown into shelves, pushed around, and punched in the stomach with combination locks. I was so scared that I became constipated for a full week. There were many opportunities for me to fight back, but we were told that if we got into one fight, we would be expelled and our parents would lose the $12,000 tuition immediately.

After the first two weeks, our parents were allowed to come and visit. My father, mother, and sister came, along with my dog. I told them everything that happened then I cried and I cried. My mother and father are both former Israeli military and all they were excited about was the fact that I had lost weight in the last two weeks. My mother didn't believe a word that I said and, while I thought that I would be going home that day, they left me there. I never fought back because I was more afraid of the consequences at home than of what would happen at the school which, in my mind now is absolutely ridiculous, but then again I was only a child then, as many bullying victims are.

Things got even worse. On the fifth day after visiting day, someone had made a mess in the bathroom and blamed me. I was told to go clean it up by several of the students and I absolutely refused. Because the true culprit never confessed, that night we were going to have to clean all of the toilet bowls with our own personal toothbrushes. You can imagine how upset everyone was and, of course, they directed it towards me. One of the other plebes felt bad for me and gave me a heads up that I was going to get a "blanket party." I had no idea what that was. I later found out that it is when a blanket is thrown over you and held down while others beat you with bars of soap and combination locks inside of socks.

I immediately went to the officer's room and barged in. They yelled at me for not knocking, but at that point I didn't care. I told them what I heard and they laughed and said that nothing would happen to me. They didn't care. In my eyes, no one did.

I understand the fear and terror that goes through a bullying victim's mind right before they make a choice that could be a terminal one. At that exact moment, in my mind, there was only one option. I walked to my room and saw my roommate and one of the other kids who had been bullying me. I opened up my closet, grabbed the first thing that I saw, which was a bottle of Brasso® (belt buckle cleaner), said, "down the hatch," and proceeded to drink it.

My roommate knocked the bottle out of my hand as I spat whatever I didn't swallow all over the floor. I was immediately rushed to the hospital. The doctor knocked me out so that he could put a scope down my throat and see how bad the damage was.

Two months later, my parents put me back into public school. There was one thing very different about me. I made a choice. And that choice was that I was never going to be bullied ever again, so I became a bully.

Chapter 1: Standing Up to the Bully

Olivia was very excited to go to her first birthday party since attending her new school. She had just started first grade and had already made a few friends. Julia, Olivia's mother, had helped Olivia pick out the perfect dress for the party. It was a dark purple dress with adorable ruffles. Soon after they knocked on the door, it opened up and a party atmosphere presented itself. Olivia saw her friend, Lucy, through the screen door and yelled to her with excitement. Lucy ran up to Olivia and hugged her the second she came inside. "Thank you for coming to my birthday party Olivia." Lucy said. "Thank you. I really like your dress," Olivia responded back politely. "You have such a lovely daughter," said the woman that opened the door. "I'm Lucy's mother, Stella."

Stella brought Julia over to meet the rest of the parents as Olivia started playing in the backyard with the rest of the children. Julia was happy that she was getting to meet some new parents in a non-work environment. As an elementary school teacher, most of the time meeting a new parent means a parent-teacher conference about their child. "This is a nice change of pace," she thought to herself. Julia struck up a conversation with another parent and, on occasion, like every parent would, glanced over towards Olivia to make sure she was okay.

Olivia was enjoying the princess-themed party and was really looking forward to going into the bouncy house. "That looks like a lot of fun," she thought. Lucy asked Olivia, "Do you want to go into the bouncy house before the pizza comes?" Olivia's eyes lit up like two twinkling stars. Since her mom

put her in Yogarate® (Yoga & Karate) two years ago,
she had always wanted to practice a jumping kick
that she saw one of her favorite cartoons do and this
was her chance. Lucy and Olivia ran over to the
bouncy house and got in the line. Olivia waited in
line excitedly as she watched the children in the
bouncy house having a great time. Her turn was
almost here. The anticipation was building up.

All of a sudden, another girl stepped in front of
Olivia and Lucy and cut the line. "Sarah, no cutting.
This is my birthday party. Wait in line like everybody
else." Sarah was a third grader who came with her
younger sister to the party. Sarah turned to Lucy and
said "Shut up!" and pushed her. Olivia was always
taught to stand up for her friends and she stepped in
front of Lucy and told Sarah to leave her alone.
When Sarah went to push Olivia, Olivia stepped to

15

the side, stuck her foot out and tripped her, just like she was trained in her Yogarate class. Immediately after Sarah hit the ground, she got up, ran to her mother and started to cry. "That girl pushed me!" Sarah said to her mother, and pointed to Olivia. Sarah's mother, completely oblivious of the situation, started heading towards the bouncy house. Julia caught this out of the corner of her eye and followed Sarah's mother.

Sarah's mother immediately started yelling at Olivia. A few seconds later, Stella and Julia arrived on the scene. Julia asked Olivia, "What happened?" Olivia responded, "That girl," pointing to Sarah, "pushed Lucy on the grass when Lucy told her not to cut the line. I told her to leave Lucy alone and she tried to push me. I did what Yensei taught me and she fell on the ground." Sarah's mother exploded. "Is that what you teach your child?" Julia calmly looked at Sarah's mother and said, "To defend herself? If that's what you're referring to, then that's exactly what we teach our children. We put her in a Yogarate® school so that she would know exactly what to do in the exact situation like this when dealing with a bully. Maybe next time, your daughter will think twice about picking on someone smaller than her." Julia put her hand out and Olivia gladly took it. They both walked away as Sarah's mother turned her anger towards Stella.

"Mommy, did I do anything wrong?" Olivia asked with a concerned look on her face. Julia squatted down, looked her in her eyes and said, "You did a wonderful job. I'm so proud of you. You stood up for your friend and you stood up to a bully bigger than you. I also know that you could have used your

Yogarate® on her and I'm very happy that you didn't." Julia smiled at Olivia and gave her an amazing hug. "Your daddy is going to be so happy to hear what happened today. I'm going to call him right now!" Julia started to dial her phone to call her husband. Being a martial artist himself, she knew he would love to hear what happened. She also knew that she needed to initiate another positive enforcer for Olivia so that this life lesson would be looked at as a positive.

Julia was certainly happy that this event didn't happen at school. As an elementary school teacher, she knew all too well about the over-abuse of Zero Tolerance laws in the schools. Olivia would have been suspended for at least three days. "How does that teach a child anything?" she thought. She remembered years ago when she was in elementary school and she got into a scuffle with another girl. She was sent immediately to the vice-principal's office. The vice-principal sat both girls down, figured out what happened and who started the fight, called both parents, and gave out a punishment to the child that started the fight. Even after all that, the other girl didn't stop picking on her. Nothing the principal or the bully's parents told her made her stop picking on Julia. Then Julia's older sister intervened and the bullying stopped immediately.

Julia watched Olivia's face light up as her father told her how proud he was of her. She barely noticed Stella until she was right behind her. "Boy, did I get an earful from Sarah's mother! I have a pretty good idea how Sarah learned to be such a good bully," Stella said and shook her head. They both made eye contact and laughed. The rest of the princess party was a smashing success... and a bully free one.

LIFE SKILLS TOOLBOX

Here and now is your first opportunity to truly have a new experience from the reading of this book. I had a parent tell me that when they answered these questions for themselves, it helped to write down the answers and take a deep breath between each question. A cleansing of the mind's palate, if you will. I invite you to answer the following questions for yourself.

Questions for self-exploration:

1. How did you feel as you read this first chapter?

2. Did you find yourself taking a particular side?

3. Was there a particular part that got your blood boiling?

4. How would you respond if you were Olivia's parent?

5. How would you respond if you were Lucy's parent?

6. How would you respond if you were Sarah's parent?

Think about how you would want your own child to behave as the bully (Sarah), the victim (Lucy), and the bystander (Olivia). This isn't a conversation about who was right and who was wrong. This is only to start trying on another person's perspective in the hopes that this skill will help your children. Imagine if you can teach your children this skill as well. Try it on, for them.

Chapter 2: Parents, Lead by Example

Olivia and her entire family came out to watch her brother's, Zachary's brown belt testing at his Yogarate® school. Zachary was sitting cross-legged on the floor with the rest of his friends, anxiously awaiting the opportunity to show his stuff. He had been practicing his kata (sequence of moves) and Sun salutations every single day for the past two weeks. He watched as Yensei (his Yogi/Sensei) worked with the white and yellow belts to help them successfully complete their test. Olivia and the other green belts were up next. Zachary had spent time practicing with Olivia. As a green belt, it was the first opportunity for the children to actually spar in their class. Julia liked the fact that the children were sparring with light contact. As a teacher, she knew that the only way to really know if something was learned is to try it and repeatedly practice it. The children were also being taught self-control, even though they were wearing foam pads on their hands, head, and feet. It boosted the children's confidence to know that what they learned in the class would actually be effective outside the class, if necessary.

During Olivia's sparring, she was kicked in the stomach a little harder than she expected. Julia could tell that this scared her, as she saw tears well up in her eyes. Yensei quickly went over to see if Olivia was okay. He squatted down next to her and waited for her to make eye contact. He asked her, "What do we do when we get scared, mad, or sad? We take a deep breath with our nose, like we're smelling flowers and breathe out with our mouth, like we're blowing out a birthday candle." He then started to demonstrate by breathing deeply through his nose and out through the mouth. After a few breaths, Olivia started breathing with him and eventually, the tears disappeared. Olivia looked around the room, slightly embarrassed and, to her surprise, saw all the children in the room breathing with her. Once again, Julia was reminded why she loved the Yogarate® program so much. She had even brought some of the breathing games and meditations that she saw her children learn into her own classroom.

Zachary and the rest of the brown belts were up next. He began his kata smoothly. At one point though, he forgot a technique and became nervous. As he stopped in the middle of his kata, he remembered what Yensei said to Olivia. Zachary took a beautiful, deep filling breath with his nose and, by the time his breath left his mouth, he remembered the technique that he forgot. He finished his kata and sat down back on his spot.

There was one child, named Harry, who had a difficult time completing his kata. Zachary had a feeling that Harry had not been practicing anywhere near as much as he had. At the end of the brown belt testing, Yensei congratulated all the children on trying their best and emphasized that whether they passed the test or not, they should be proud of themselves for doing their best. Harry was the only child out of the five that did not pass his test. When he found out he wasn't going to advance to his brown belt, Harry started crying and ran to his mother.

Zachary felt bad for him but he also knew how hard he had been practicing and he felt that if Harry would have practiced just as long, then he would have been able to advance to the next belt. Julia went over to Zachary after the testing was over and gave him a big hug. Dad gave him a high five and told him how proud he was of him. As the congratulations were going around, Zachary saw Harry's mother raising her voice to Yensei. Zachary tried to listen in and he was surprised at what he heard. Zachary's mother said that she thought that Harry should get his brown belt like everybody else. She mentioned that in school, everybody wins, and it hurt Harry's feelings that he didn't get his brown belt. Yensei looked at her and said, "What happens at your school and what happens at this dojo are two different things. My job is to ensure that your children get the best possible training for life through these classes. I understand that in their schools, things have changed and now children are receiving prizes no matter how hard they work. However, that's not how life works. Harry is going to face disappointment in his life and if you coddle him instead of supporting him in learning these valuable life lessons, then what kind of adult do you think he's going to grow up to be? Why would he try harder at anything if he's going to get a prize no matter how hard he works?"

Harry's mother was taken aback and didn't believe what she was hearing. "I don't want to hear him whining to me that he didn't get his brown belt." Yensei smiled at her and said, "And therein lies the truth. This isn't about Harry and his brown belt. This is about you not wanting to hear him whine. And, instead of having him take responsibility for his actions, and showing him why he needs to practice more, you're trying to manipulate me into giving him a brown belt that he did not earn. Nice try," Yensei said with a softer smile. He knew that this moment to possibly help her needed to be handled delicately. "Our job as adults is to teach children how to be prepared for life as adults. What are you teaching your child right now? And please know that you are not the first parent, nor will you be the last, that comes to me with this concern. Remember that we're both on the same team and want Harry to grow up to be a good man. I'd like you to consider two questions that will make a massive difference in both of your lives. Are you ready?"

It took a lot for her to swallow her pride as she thought about it, and then said, "I'm ready, but I don't think I'm about to like what you have to say." Yensei warmly smiled and asked, "What is more important for you? To have your child like you or respect you? Another way to ask that question is: are you more interested in being your child's friend or their parent? You can't be both." She was taken aback by what he said. It wasn't that he was offending her. It was that he had hit home 100% and she felt that in her body. When she was growing up, her mother was very strict with her and she remembered getting a whooping one time for lying about cheating on a test in school. She ran to her room crying and she remembered saying to herself, "When I have kids, I'm not going to be mean to them like mom was mean to me." She thought back and giggled a little bit. Her mother didn't care if she liked her but she sure made sure she respected her.

Right then and there, she looked at Yensei and said, "Thank you so much for being so honest with me. Not many people would say that to me. What do

I do now?" He looked at her with warmth in his eyes and said, "Right here and now, make a choice to be his parent and not his friend. That doesn't mean that you can't be friendly with him, but you need to understand that he will test you. If you give in to his whining or another behavior that you don't approve of, like being disrespectful, then what life lesson has he learned and how will he be as a teenager and then as an adult? Right here and now, declare to be his mother and his disciplinarian. Say it. I am his mother and his disciplinarian and I love him." She said those exact words out loud and a sensation of warmth and power filled her whole body like she'd never felt before. Day one of being super mom began.

LIFE SKILLS TOOLBOX

Questions for self-exploration:

1. How was this chapter for you?

2. Whose side did you take?

3. Did you take the Yensei's side or did it offend you?

4. Did you relate with Harry's mother?

5. Are you tired of hearing children whine about something that they didn't get?

6. Did they not get it because they weren't prepared?

7. Did YOU not get something you wanted at some point in your life because you were not prepared?

As humans introduced to a new scenario, we usually take a side when we see a conversation or argument take place. Some people displace feelings that they have towards themselves onto others so that they can get a temporary sensation of relief as they shift responsibility off of themselves and onto another person. For you to truly help the children in your life, you get to make a choice right this moment. The choice is simple. Will you throw away your responsibility as an intelligent adult and make this book about YOU or will you make this book about helping to prevent and eventually eliminate bullying in your environment, whether it is at school, in public, or at home? The great thing about choice is that you get to re-choose over and over again.

Harry's mother unknowingly chose herself initially and then, at the end of the chapter, chose Harry. She

33

can re-choose all day and night. Today, you can be the champion for all children and open your mind to the concepts in this book and tomorrow you may choose that your own life's sob stories are more important than your commitment as an educator, parent, or both. And either way works! You choose. Ultimately, the way bullying is dealt with around you, and the people in your life, is up to you. What will you choose?

Chapter 3: The Bully: Why Bullies Bully

Sarah woke up to the sounds of her parents yelling at each other. As the sun beamed in from the window, she yawned as she rubbed her eyes gently. She wondered to herself what this morning's argument was all about. Yesterday's argument was about Daddy forgetting to pay something. The day before, it was about Mommy forgetting something at the supermarket. Sarah didn't want to go downstairs while the shouting was happening, so she decided to read a book and wait. The last thing she heard her mom yell was, "Why can't you just tell your boss 'no' when he wants you to work on Saturday? Now I have to take the girls to this birthday party all by myself. Thanks a lot!" she finished, in a sarcastic tone.

After 10 minutes of quiet, Sarah slowly strolled down the stairs and had a seat at the kitchen table. Her little sister sat at the table already eating her food. The yelling didn't seem to bother her. Maybe it was all the excitement of going to the party that had tuned out the yelling. Mom and Dad weren't talking to each other, so Sarah sat in the awkward quiet. Dad sat at the table and finished his breakfast quickly. He placed the dishes in the sink, walked over to Sarah, and gave her a kiss on her forehead. He then walked over to her sister and said, "Have fun at the birthday party, honey," and walked out of the kitchen.

Sarah could see that her mom was still upset. She knew that when she got like that, it wasn't a good idea to ask her any questions. Sarah quietly ate her breakfast and daydreamed of happy horses running around in a wide-open field. As she finished her breakfast, she figured now was the best time to ask the question that was bothering her. "Mommy," she began, "why do I have to go to the birthday party? I want to stay home and play with my friends here." Sarah immediately regretted asking that question when saw her mother's face turn bright red. "Your father was too afraid to tell his boss no, so he had to go to work and leave me with both of you! All I am telling you is you better behave at the birthday party or you're going to be in big trouble!" her mother yelled at her. Sarah was so shocked and surprised by what just happened that she ran upstairs crying and yelled, "I don't want to go to the stupid party anyway!"

After the telling off from her mother, Sarah finally got dressed and dragged herself downstairs. She saw her little sister running around excited about the party and got even more upset. She wanted to push her or do something else to get her to stop having fun. "That would make me feel better," she thought to herself. The car ride to the party was even worse. By the time they got there, Sarah was ready to explode. As the front door opened, Sarah and her sister ran inside the house. There was the sound of music and laughter coming from the backyard. As she went outside, Sarah observed happy children jumping in a bounce house and focused on two girls laughing in the line. She needed to get rid of the pain she was feeling inside. Sarah thought back to her mother screaming at her and felt small, helpless, and unsafe. She needed to get rid of that feeling, immediately. She charged straight towards the girls and cut right in front of them.

LIFE SKILLS TOOLBOX

1. Who is around you when you are having a heated discussion or a full-on argument?

2. Do you ever notice that your children watch you and learn to take on your arguing/negotiation skills?

Sometimes we win arguments and sometimes we don't. And it never helps if the person we are arguing with doesn't respond back with the same passion in the argument. We make up stories in our minds to justify our point like, "They don't care enough to argue!" Whenever we lose an argument that bullied/loss of power feeling creeps up and takes over until we feed it by making someone else feel bad. It can be with a rude remark or straight on bullying.

I invite you to take some time for yourself and think about times in your life that you reacted in a way that did not benefit you. Looking at those instances, try on that you are the only person who can control your emotions AND how you respond to other people. If someone says something mean to you, the average adult thinks that they got upset because of the words and actions of the other person. However if they said the exact same words to you in a language you didn't speak, then you wouldn't feel bad, upset or bullied at all because those emotions and feelings are all created from your perception and interpretation of what was said. If you don't 100% understand this, it's quite okay. I didn't either at first and had to ask for clarification. I invite you to reread this entire passage again until you get how powerful you are.

Do you see that no one can upset or bully you without your consent? If you do, here comes the kicker. Ever since you were born, no one has ever "made you feel bad." No one has ever "upset you." No one has ever bullied you. You, as I did when I was 12, allowed your own mind to give power to others in your life and hand the responsibility of your happiness to others.

When you, as an adult, feel a loss of power because someone "made you feel bad" then you get sucked into an ongoing cycle of trying to relieve your self-created upset by making someone else feel bad and instantly feeling better about yourself. The problem is that you just created a bullying victim who may become a bully and ruin someone else's day by bullying them. They, in turn, become a victim and then bully someone else and so on. If you are a selfish person, that's 100% OK and you have every right to live your life any way that works for you, no matter what most people in society say.

That statement wasn't meant to be a put down and I need to clarify that. Being 100% selfish works for some people and they are happy with their lives. If, however, you have any interest in choosing to be a person who has consideration for others and is aware of what consequences your own actions could have on other people, including the children in your life, then I invite you to think about a situation when you responded to a child in a way that you could see in their face that they were upset, scared or distraught. What happened after the child left the area? Did you feel better? Do you feel better now that you are thinking about it? How do you think the child felt? Did you hear about any unusual aggressive behaviors from that child's school or another adult close to them?

If you choose to be powerful and you want the same for your children, then you can choose to stop children from being upset by having a clean-up conversation with them consisting of understanding how they feel, explaining why you responded the way you did, sincerely apologizing to the child and promising that you'll do your best to never let it happen again. Then, and only then, will you prove yourself as their champion by interfering and stopping their mind from turning them into a bully. You, the reader, right now can POWERFULLY CHOOSE that, from this moment forward, you are the only one that chooses your happiness and how you respond to everyone and everything else in your life. Will you give your boss, spouse, or children power over you or will you choose to be your own superhero from this day forward? Oh... and not choosing is still making a choice. ;)

Chapter 4: "Teachers Don't Bully!"

Zachary and his friend Thomas were still excited about their brown belt test the next day as they discussed it on the bus ride to school. They were talking about getting their black belts soon and this caught the interest of an older boy named Billy. As they all got off the bus at school, Billy went up to Zachary and asked him if he thought he was a tough guy because he was taking Yogarate®. Zachary could sense the sarcasm and read Billy's body language as being very aggressive. Zachary looked up at the older boy and said to him politely, "Please leave us alone." They immediately walked away, as Billy stood there making fun of them.

Zachary had forgotten about the incident in the morning until it was time to go home and he got on the bus. Billy was sitting in the back and immediately started antagonizing him. Zachary chose to sit in the front and Thomas sat next to him. Billy came all the way up to the front of the bus and sat behind the boys. Billy started to flick Zachary's ears and continued to poke fun at him. The bus finally got to his stop and he got off and ran home. Julia opened the door and greeted him with a smile. Zachary told her what had happened that morning and then on the bus ride home. Julia told him that he did a wonderful job of telling her and she would call the school tomorrow.

The next morning, Julia called the principal's office as she was driving to her school. The principal's secretary answered the phone and, when Julia asked to speak to the principal, the secretary asked her what it was in reference to. Although she really wanted to speak to the principal, she explained the situation to the secretary and was then directed to the principal's voice mail. Julia left a brief message simply requesting that he contact her back regarding her son being bullied. She left her cell phone number for the principal's convenience. Lunchtime came around and there were no calls or voice-mails from the principal. Julia tried calling the school again and the same secretary answered. This time, the secretary gave her an attitude and told her, "The principal will get back to you when he gets back to you. He is a very busy man." Julia requested the principal's voice mail again and after she was transferred, left a lengthy and descriptive voice mail detailing all the information of the events of the previous day. As the school day came to a close,

Julia got more and more upset that she had not received any phone calls from anyone at the school.

Zachary arrived home soon after Julia and told her that Billy was still bothering him. As she saw the worry in her son's eyes, she promised him that she would call again tomorrow and if not, she would actually go into his school. The next morning, Julia called the school again and to her dismay, discovered the same secretary on the other end of the line. Before Julia could even get a word out, the secretary snapped at her and said, "Lady, you left a voice mail for the principal and he'll get back to you when he gets back to you. Don't call back here until you hear from him," and she hung up. Julia was furious. She couldn't believe the way that the secretary spoke to her and then hung up. She was so upset that she tried to take a sip of her coffee to calm herself down.

Unfortunately, that didn't help. Julia got to her school still upset and didn't realize she brought her feelings into her classroom.

With every period that passed, Julia got more upset. "How could she speak to me like that?" she thought. "The nerve of that lady!" Julia decided that she would drive over to the school during her lunch break. She couldn't stand the thought of telling Zachary that nothing had changed, again. With fifteen minutes of class left, Julia's frustration was building. She had given her class an assignment to work on and had noticed a few times that Dale, who sat in the back row, was whispering to his neighbor instead of working. She had had enough of people undermining her and taking advantage of her. She stood up and stomped over to Dale's seat. As her emotions overwhelmed her, her face reddened and she lost her temper. "WHY CAN'T YOU JUST BE QUIET AND DO YOUR WORK LIKE EVERYONE ELSE IN CLASS!?! STOP WHISPERING AND FINISH YOUR ASSIGNMENT!!" she yelled. Julia turned around and stomped over to her desk. She sat down abruptly and stared at the clock on the wall. She wanted to go. She wanted to scream at the secretary who was so unbelievably rude to her.

Dale was in total shock. As Julia towered over him and continued to scream, he tried to keep his composure. "I was only whispering to Allen. Why on earth is she flipping out like this?" he thought to himself. He thought about how his mother would scream at him like that when she had a bad day. "Ms. Julia is soooo mean," he thought. For the next 15 minutes, Dale seemed to get more and more upset. His thoughts hopped from Ms. Julia screaming at him, to his mother, to his younger sister, who would yell at him to feel better after their mom yelled at her. When the bell rang, he grabbed his lunch from his cubby and started walking fast towards the door with his head down. Julia tried to get his attention by calling his name, but he intentionally ignored her and ran down the hallway towards the cafeteria. He was still upset about the events from the last period. As he ran the experience back over and over and over in his mind, his body felt different. As he got madder, his frustration turned to rage. His upset turned into sadness. His chest felt like someone had put a bowling ball on it and left a large, gaping hole. He felt incomplete. He felt hurt and angry and sad, and didn't know how to stop the pain. He just wanted it to stop.

As Dale walked with his head down, he accidentally bumped shoulders with a boy walking in the opposite direction. The emotions hit their boiling point. Dale spun around, raised both his hands, and shoved the boy onto the ground as hard as possible. Immediately after the boy hit the ground, the pain went away. It disappeared. Completely and amazingly, a sense of peace and balance came over Dale. He felt whole again and let go of everything and anything he had been upset about. He had his power back... until the next time he gets bullied.

LIFE SKILLS TOOLBOX

Questions for self-exploration:

1. Do you ever find yourself stuck in the tight grasp of the bullying circle?
2. Can you do anything about it when you are in the middle of getting bullied or being a bully?

3. Can you do anything about it after the bullying moment has passed?

4. What role can you play in breaking the bullying circle?

5. Who can you stand up to that bullies you?

6. Who can you choose to stop bullying?

Be a **S.T.A.R.** for your children. **Stop, Think, Act** and **Review**. Why I see parents and teachers telling their children to stop crying, relax, or take a deep breath whenever they are upset boggles my mind because if they were in that exact situation and another adult told them to stop crying, relax, or take a deep breath, they would instantly get even more upset. If it doesn't work for you, it won't work for your children.

In the event that you feel like you are getting bullied by another and you haven't embraced the previous chapter's conversation that "no one can get you upset... responsibility... Blah blah blah" (you aren't the only one), then I invite you to **Stop**, **Think** about what happened, choose to **Act** in a different way and **Review** the situation to see if the way you handled it worked better or if you could handle it differently next time. Be their **STAR**!

Chapter 5: The Principals, Captains of the Ships

After repeated phone calls to the principal's office, the only response that she received was, "We will get back to you," Julia decided that it was time for her to go to the office herself and find out what was really happening. She walked into the principal's office and demanded to see Mr. Phillips, the principal. Being a seasoned teacher, she knew that all she had to do was sit around long enough and he would see her. The door to the principal's office finally opened up and he reluctantly waved her in. She sensed by his body language that he was not happy to see her. As she sat down, Mr. Phillips began the conversation with, "You're really supposed to make an appointment to see me."

She could feel already what he was trying to do and she did not respond to that statement. She began the conversation with kindness. She knew that any other way would not get her the results that she was looking for. "I really appreciate the time that you're giving me as I know your schedule is very busy." Even though she wanted to mention that she had left multiple messages with his secretary, she knew that would just throw kindling on the fire and what she wanted to do was figure out a way to help stop her son from being bullied, not become the principal's bullying victim.

Instead, she started the conversation with, "My son is getting picked on on the school bus and he's told the bus driver, but it seems like nothing is changing and he is still getting picked on. What do you suggest?" Mr. Phillips tried to look surprised;

however, she could tell by his facial expressions that he already knew about this situation. Mr. Phillips responded, "I will look into this and get back to you as soon as I see what the situation is." Julia wasn't too optimistic, but what choice did she have? She had to go through the proper channels and this was the first step. As Julia closed the door behind her, the principal began to think about the current situation and was stuck.

What Julia didn't know was that the child that was bullying Zachary had been involved in a bullying situation last year. Billy attacked a younger student. Mr. Phillips suspended Billy and unfortunately had to suspend the boy that Billy hit because of the abuse of Zero Tolerance laws. He cringed as he remembered the heated conversation with Billy's parents as they yelled and screamed at him about how he and the school were discriminating against their son. As he sat there taking their verbal onslaught, he completely understood where their child picked up his learned bullying skills. He imagined the mother and father using the same tone of voice on each other while Billy sat, quietly observing and learning their behaviors to then practice them at school. Unfortunately those parents didn't have the knowledge or clarity to take responsibility for their son's actions, so instead, they complained and threatened and bullied until the final victim, the superintendent, caved in from fear.

The parents demanded that they speak to the superintendent immediately because Mr. Phillips was not responding to the yelling, the demands, or the threats of lawsuits from Billy's parents. He knew the family and knew they couldn't afford the hours and hours an attorney would cost for a case like this, yet they claimed they would sue everyone. A day later, Mr. Phillips received a call from the superintendent's office to, "leave Billy alone." The bully had won. When he asked for clarification, all he got was a bunch of inauthentic mumbo-jumbo that was full of statements like "Threats of litigation...the district doesn't need...call it a misunderstanding...apology to Billy's parents...in hopes this will go away." He shook his head in utter disappointment.

He remembered when he was a vice-principal years ago and, when a fight broke out, the attacker received a negative consequence and the victim was taken care of and supported. Now the victim is punished alongside the bully. "We are supposed to be teaching our children how to function and excel in the adult world, yet we are reinforcing the complete

59

opposite. If I was in public and was assaulted and I defended myself, I wouldn't get in trouble. The police officer would arrive and ask me if I wanted to press charges on the attacker. Would I be arrested because the police didn't want to take responsibility for actually looking into the crime and doing the work needed to solve the case? Of course not. Then why is it OK in our schools?" Mr. Phillips shook his head, knowing that if he even mentioned anything to Billy's parents than Pandora's Box would open up again and he couldn't risk losing his job just for one child. "I'll figure out a way to keep them separated," he thought to himself. "I hope this works. It has to." Now he just had to figure out how to handle Julia and not say anything specific that would get him in trouble in the future.

Zachary came home that next day crying. "Billy was picking on me again today. I told the bus driver and he told me to go sit somewhere else, so I did. Billy then got out of his seat and came over to me and started picking on me again. The bus driver did nothing to stop it. When I told him to leave me alone, he started pushing me in my seat. I don't want to go to school anymore!" he cried. Mom had to handle this conversation very delicately. She remembered when she was younger and how she was picked on by two girls one grade above her. Luckily, her older sister found out that she was getting picked on and beat up the two bullies herself. The entire school heard about what happened and she was never bullied ever again. "It's amazing how differently we handle things now," she thought to herself. Back then, if I had a problem, I would go to my parents or teacher for help. They would listen to me and then give me real life suggestions based on their real life experience. These days, parents and teachers have to constantly monitor and filter themselves when having conversations with anyone, especially each other.

Julia remembered a conversation she had with a parent, during which she suggested that the parent spend more time reading with their child. Instead of the parent taking some responsibility for her child and being open to the suggestion from the teacher, she got offended and complained to her principal, Mr. Harris. Instead of the principal backing her up and agreeing with her, he immediately agreed with the parent and reprimanded her. Her own principal tried to explain to her that she needed to be more caring and considerate of the feelings of the parents and try not to say things that might offend them. "How do you do that?" she asked? "How do you expect me to be able to read the mind of another adult and know what will offend them? You are literally asking the impossible."

Mr. Harris sat in silence for a few moments. She could tell he was actually thinking about what she said. As he took a deep breath, his face softened and he said, "I don't know. I don't know how I can ask you to do that. I agree; it doesn't make sense. I've been the principal here for over 20 years and I don't know how things have shifted to the point that we constantly have to be on our toes and worried about offending everyone else. I remember having conversations with teachers and parents and yes, sometimes they got heated. Voices are raised when passionate people have differences of opinions.

Especially when the education and wellness of a child is at stake. Sometimes people's feelings were hurt. It was up to the adult to realize it was their feelings that were hurt and they would take responsibility for dealing with their emotions. This generation of adults does not want to take responsibility. Instead, somehow, we now throw blame on everyone else to avoid our own responsibility. The worst thing is that, when we throw away our responsibility, we don't realize that we throw away our power as well."

"Do you realize that we, as adults, have manipulated the English language so that we do not have to be responsible for choices that we made in the past? Just last week, I had a teacher here complaining to me about how another teacher "pressured" her into changing her schedule and switching shifts for cafeteria duty. I wanted to tell that teacher, 'That never happened. You could have told her "no" and you didn't. You chose not to stand up for yourself and say "no" and instead of accepting that responsibility, you are coming to me to complain about her when all she did was ask you a question.' One generation ago, I could have said that and it would have been over. We would have then talked about the real problem and how to empower them. Now, if I say something like that to a teacher, then she might get "offended" and go over my head and I would get reprimanded."

As the conversation continued, the energy in the room grew. There was a sense of calm as Mr. Harris slowly reconnected with his true self. The self that had him one day choose to become an educator. "It is nearly impossible for me to do my job to the best of my ability these days. I deal with bullying situations all the time. I feel for these children and I want to help them all. Unfortunately, some of these bullies pick up their bullying characteristics from home. I learn this very quickly when I ask a parent of a child accused of being a bully to come in for a meeting. The same thing with avoiding responsibility happens with these parents as well. Instead of taking responsibility, they immediately get upset and threaten to go over my head to the superintendent's office and threaten to pursue litigation. That's the key word, threaten, a.k.a. bully.

The bottom line is that the bully's parents bully the principal and the superintendent with, typically, empty threats of litigation and the whole system crumbles. What do I tell a teacher when she removes a child from her classroom for being a bully and expects an action to be taken by us to deter and eliminate the behavior? Then, instead of teaching that bully that these behaviors will not be acceptable, that it comes with consequences, I have no choice but to return them to the same classroom in which he was disruptive in the first place. The only way to stop a bully is to stand up to a bully with help from others. The day I can truly help the teachers eliminate bullying in their classrooms is the day that schools take a stand for themselves and stand up to these bullying parents. And starting right now I am going to think about what is best for our students first. I, right now, choose to take a stand to protect them from bullies by standing up to bullies myself!"

Julia left her principal's office in a state of pure awe. Mr. Harris completely laid it out for her. The bullying in schools affects the students, teachers, principals, and parents alike. She was absolutely amazed at how he had changed in front of her eyes. "If one principal can change," she thought, "then they can all change. All they have to do is choose to take the responsibility for their students' safety and education once again. When they take on the responsibility, they get back the power." Remembering that experience vividly like it just happened, Julia was ready to walk back into Mr. Phillip's door and help him change...that is...if he would choose to.

LIFE SKILLS TOOLBOX

Mr. Phillips was put into a tremendously difficult situation. A situation where he had to decide between two difficult decisions. As we go through life, we think that we make choices when, in fact, we make decisions. In a seminar called, "The Landmark Forum," that I attended, I learned the difference between choices and decisions. The root of the word "decide" is "cide". Other words that have that root are suicide, homicide, and genocide. It means the act of killing. So, whenever you decide, or make a decision, you are doing it based on killing off some other option. Do you decide what restaurants to go to or what movie to see based on previous experience, the opinions of others and other factors? Or do you really choose to go to a restaurant simply to go to that restaurant?

Mr. Phillips was smack dab in the vortex of the bullying circle and he didn't even know it. And, just like in real life, the threats of bullies are rarely backed up by the bully and usually come from a place of weakness and fear. It amazes me how afraid our society has become when someone just uses the words, "I'll sue you," and everyone scatters like cockroaches when the light turns on. I understand that no one wants to be sued. Do most people think about how expensive attorneys are and how most people don't have the $300 to $500 an hour to pay for these attorneys? Based on conversations I've had with attorneys that have worked for the schools and against them, the odds are very slim to none that an attorney will take on one of these cases pro-bono. Yet, instead of standing up to the bullies, or in this situation, the parents of the accused bully, we give in and continue the bullying circle from superintendent to principal to vice-principal to teacher to students and parents.

General Norman Schwarzkopf said, "When given the opportunity to lead, lead." And, "When leading, do what's right."

Take a deep breath and give up believing that you were ever pressured into doing anything. It never happened, you are too smart and powerful to believe that anymore, choose this moment, right now, to take 100% responsibility for every choice and decision that you have ever made and declare that from this moment on, you are a champion for your children.

What would a champion do when faced with the next situation? Will you handle it like a victim or like a champion? The choice is yours.

Chapter 6: The Victim

Billy continued to pick on Zachary. Zachary knew that it wasn't OK to hit Billy just because he was making fun of him. Yensei always said, "Mental Yogarate® for mental attacks, physical Yogarate® for physical attacks." Zachary didn't understand why the bullying wasn't stopping. He had told his mother twice and she always did what she said she would do. Julia called ahead to the dojo to let them know she was running late to pick up Zachary from Yogarate®. Yensei told him that he could wait in the front office with him if he liked. He had noticed that Zachary wasn't being his normal chipper self in class and was showing signs of being upset. Yensei's belly started to vibrate and he knew to listen immediately.

They both sat down in the office and Yensei asked him if there was anything wrong.

Zachary shook his head no and turned away. This was very odd behavior coming from one of his happiest students. Yensei knew that Zachary's wall was up and his mind wasn't allowing him to simply tell him what the problem was. Yensei took a breath and prepared to do a brain kata in Zachary's mind. This was the **CAP** (**Connect, Another, Praise**) kata. First, he needed to **CONNECT** with his student so that they both understood what it was like to be in Zachary's shoes in that exact moment. He needed to use visual and kinesthetic phrasing to **CONNECT** with him on a more emotional level. "Zachary, I **see** that you are upset about something and that's OK. Sometimes I **feel** like saying something to someone or asking for help and I can't do it." There was a moment of silence that felt longer than it was. Zachary looked over at Yensei and could genuinely get that he knew and understood what he was feeling. A feeling of flowing energy began between teacher and student. Yensei saw this, took another deep breath and continued the kata. Right before he was about to speak, Zachary took a deep breath.

"I have **ANOTHER** boy in **ANOTHER** class, who has the same hair color and sneakers like yours." Yensei said as he watched Zachary's eyes as they darted up and to his right as he created a mental picture of that boy. Yensei knew that the picture of the boy he created looked like Zachary. "Now it is time to take Zachary's mind's focus away from Zachary," he thought. "This little boy's name is Max and I think that he wants to share something with me and I think that he would feel better if he did.

Maybe you can help me help Max?" Zachary turned towards him and nodded his head in intrigue. "I can't think like a little kid, but you can. What kind of things do boys your age get upset about? What do you think is getting Max so angry and scared?" Zachary looked at Yensei and blurted out, "Maybe there is a bigger boy picking on him on the bus?" Without skipping a beat, Yensei continued asking him questions about the bullying situation and Zachary talked openly without his mind's filter kicking in.

After Yensei got the entire story, he finished the CAP kata with some **PRAISE**. "Zachary, thank you for helping me understand Max better. I am going to speak with him next time I see him and I'll tell him what to do to stop the bigger boy from picking on him so that he can feel better." Yensei stood up and gave him a high five and told him of the great job that he did. Now he just had to wait for Zachary's mind to go through the steps it needed to until he would come back for help. When Julia pulled up outside the school, Yensei let Zachary know she was here. Yensei quickly went outside and told Julia about what he found out and that he thinks Zachary is getting bullied on the bus. Julia tried to create a smile and said, "We just found out about it and have been talking to the principal to get it to stop." Yensei smiled and wished her a good evening. Julia couldn't bear to mention that her attempts to help her son haven't proven effective yet. Then Zachary came out of the dojo and got in the car. Julia asked how class was and he responded "OK".

LIFE SKILLS TOOLBOX

CAPing a child is a great way to truly see what is bothering them without having the child's inner wall come crashing down when you ask them something personal. I invite you to try this technique when you are trying to solve the problem of a child or an adult in your life.

CAP. Connect, Another, Praise.

Connect by getting into their world and truly trying to understand how they are feeling. Help them know that you understand what they are feeling.

Another child/adult can be used that resembles the person with the problem. Ask them for help with the other person.

Praise them for helping you.

Chapter 7: Community Involvement

The bullying continued and Julia received a phone call from one of Zachary's teachers, concerned about his lack of focus in class and a change in the quality of his school work. "It doesn't seem like Zachary wants to be in school at all. This is completely not like him," mentioned his teacher. The principal didn't return her phone calls and when she reached out to the superintendent's office, she was told someone would look into it and get back to her. Julia needed to think outside the box and go outside the school to get help. She had read about a town in Monona, Wisconsin, that implemented a town ordinance holding the parents of bullies accountable for the repeated bullying actions of their child. Julia contacted the township office and was transferred to

Sergeant Murphy, the police officer that suggested and followed through with the ordinance. Julia was excited to ask him many questions and he was happy to answer them.

Sergeant Murphy told her about how he went to a training on how to stop bullying and they addressed the lack of parental accountability and involvement in the lives and actions that some bullies take. He proposed a monetary fine on parents of bullies who were repeat offenders, in school or out. The township proposed it and it passed. (This is a fact.) They now have an ordinance that defines bullying as, "an intentional course of conduct which is reasonably likely to intimidate, emotionally abuse, slander, threaten, or intimidate another person and which serves no legitimate purpose." The tickets are a municipal code violation, not a criminal offense. Julia thanked him for his time and was excited to bring this idea to her township. "If we can keep the school from getting involved, we can actually stop bullying by getting the parents of the bullies to take action when it hits their wallet," she thought proudly.

The next day she contacted the mayor's office to see who she should speak to regarding the first steps in trying to make this ordinance happen. The mayor's secretary took down her information and told her that someone would get back to her as soon as possible. A few hours later, Julia received a voicemail to contact Mrs. Parker, who was a councilwoman and liaison to the school system. Immediately, Julia shook her head and said to herself, "This is exactly what I didn't want to happen." With some hesitation, Julia picked up the phone and called Mrs. Parker. Nobody answered the phone so Julia left a lengthy message describing what she was looking to do. Two days later Mrs. Parker called back and scheduled a time for a phone meeting. *(The following conversation is an actual conversation that I personally had when I wanted to have this ordinance considered in the town I live in)*

The meeting started with Mrs. Parker explaining how she got Julia's voice mail and started doing some research amongst the three schools to see what the situation was with bullying. Mrs. Parker said, "After speaking with the administration at the schools, they let me know that they do not have a bullying problem in any of the schools so this ordinance wouldn't be necessary." Julia was immediately taken back. How can she, as a person in a role of authority representing other people, actually say that there is no bullying at any of the schools? In addition to her own situation, Julia knew of two other parents who had been having problems with bullies in their schools. One was happening right on the football field in front of the coaches, without any consequences.

Luckily, Julia had time to do her research too and took out the state report that was required to be displayed according to the new Anti-Bullying Bill of Rights law. "Mrs. Parker, this report put out by the state says that our town has three times the amount of bullying as our other neighboring towns. How can the schools say that there is no bullying when these statistics came from the reports that teachers themselves wrote about bullying situations in the schools?" Mrs. Parker immediately responded back proudly, "That is because our teachers are very good at writing their reports." Julia expected to have an interesting conversation, but this had her absolutely flabbergasted. She knew that at that very moment, there were children who were terrified to go to school and were making themselves physically sick because the adults that promised to protect them were not doing so. And this lady's main purpose for the conversation was to win a verbal argument.

If that didn't boggle Julia's mind enough, then the next few statements were the icing on the cake. "We also did some research and discovered that the parents of these bullies would not be happy if there was a fine, as it would increase their financial hardship. We did give some thought towards some kind of consequence, like possibly having the parent come in and cover a detention, but then that would upset them also," Mrs. Parker responded. Julia had enough! "Of course it would upset them! It's a fine.

Why are you so concerned about upsetting people as opposed to taking care of children who could possibly experience extreme consequences if not helped?" Mrs. Parker ended the conversation quickly and let her know that there was nothing that she could do. Julia didn't know what to do.

Everyone was so concerned about offending someone or upsetting someone that they totally threw aside every last strand of power and responsibility that they had. Julia didn't know what to do.

LIFE SKILLS TOOLBOX

Questions for self-exploration:

1. How do you feel about parents being accountable for their children's actions?

2. Other than being afraid of losing one's job, what could be another reason why you think the councilwoman responded the way she did?

3. If you are a parent, how do you feel listening to Mrs. Parker give her responses?

4. If you are an educator, how do you feel listening to Mrs. Parker give her responses?

5. Why do we, as humans, act in ways that diminish how powerful and wonderful we can be?

6. Why do you think school officials/representatives feel like they have to defend their school even if it means lying and turning a blind eye to the truth?

7. How did you feel when Mrs. Parker mentioned that consequences put on the bully's family would upset them?

Do these questions bring up some internal conflict between what is right and what is not? We respond immediately to situations that bring us stress with a typical fight or flight action. The most successful salespeople understand that when a prospect says no, they are saying no to the product or service the salesperson is trying to sell them, not the actual human being that is the salesperson. When you approach someone who is a potential mate, you ask them out and they say no, are they saying no to you as the human or simply no to the request of the date?

When you read certain parts of this book and I mention something about a parent or teacher or principal, are you taking it personally, as if you are under attack, or are you open to being truthful with yourself, admitting that you might have had some of the same thoughts and situations arise yourself? You are whole, perfect and complete. That's all. You don't need to defend yourself or create opinions about how others should and shouldn't be. Remember that the more you read and the more emotions that get stirred up, the more you care and your passion rises.

Your choice is to use that passion to pretend everything is OK and fall back into line with sheople (people who blindly follow others like sheep) or you can find areas in your life and school and home that you, as a super hero and champion for children, know is wrong and fight! Fight for the ones that can't. Fight for the children who learn not to fight for themselves. Fight for the victims and their families against the bullies and the bullying their parents do. Fight for our society as a whole, be honest with yourself, see what can be done, feel your passion

bubble and take action!

Chapter 8: How to Help Bullies and Victims

Zachary was walking through the school hallway with his friend Jesse on the way to the cafeteria. Jesse had noticed that Zachary had been acting differently over the last few weeks. Zachary was looking over his shoulder a lot. He didn't want to go outside for recess and chose to get extra help from his math teacher although he knew math was his best subject. After school, Jesse decided to go home with Zachary. They both got onto the bus and sat down in the middle row. Jesse asked Zachary if he got any new video games. Zachary wasn't paying attention and was nervously looking outside the window. His eyes darted left and right repeatedly. When Jesse asked him again, Zachary didn't answer and kept looking around. The bus door closed and the bus pulled away. Jesse noticed the immediate relief on Zachary's face. When they got to Zachary's house, they went right upstairs to his room. They played video games for a little while until they heard the door open downstairs. Julia came upstairs and said hello to them both. "Are you boys hungry?" she asked. Zachary exclaimed, "Yes!" Jesse wasn't surprised as he remembered Zachary didn't eat much of his food at lunch.

Julia came upstairs with sandwiches and juice boxes. She told them both that she had spoken to Yensei at the dojo about the bullying at Zachary's school. Since the school wasn't going to address or fix the problem, she reached out to the public library and they agreed to host a workshop that Saturday. Julia posted the event on the local Facebook parent groups and the library advertised through their newsletter. That Saturday morning, 30 families showed up with their kids in the large meeting room.

Yensei began the program by thanking everyone for attending and addressed the parents first. "Ladies and gentlemen, imagine that you're driving to work in the morning and you make the perfect cup of tea or coffee. The sweetener is just right and the temperature is ideal. As you're driving to work, you get to an area where people are trying to merge onto the road that you are on. As you get to the merge, you see on your right a nice lady waving to you to see if you would let her in. You're having a wonderful day and she smiles at you and does the hand signal requesting to go in front of you so you decide to let her go in front of you. Everybody's happy and everyone's having a great day. Now it's the next day and as you're driving to work, somebody cuts you off and makes you spill some of your coffee or tea. How do you feel right then? Are you still in the same good mood or are you feeling differently? What are your thoughts about the person who cut you off? How deep does that emotion go in your body?

Now, imagine that you get to that same exact merge and it just so happens that the same lady is waving to you and asking you if she can go in front of you again. You are still upset about the person cutting you off and now that upset is felt inside your entire body. What would you do now? Would you still let her in just like you did yesterday or would you take a different action?" The parents in the room laughed and one parent said, "I'd tap the gas pedal to stop them from getting in front of me." Other parents nodded in agreement. Yensei continued,

"Most people might tap the accelerator and not let them in and then immediately feel gratified and better about themselves. Unfortunately, now the person that you didn't let in feels upset and the bullying circle continues. The person that cut you off was the initial bully, and you felt like a victim because you were upset and couldn't get your psychological power back. So now you have the opportunity to gain back your power by not letting the other person in which immediately makes you feel better. In your mind, you are back in homeostasis. Except now you unintentionally just created a bully who will now respond or react differently because of the way you treated them. That is the bully victim circle.

A bully doesn't wake up in the morning and choose to bully someone. Something triggers them to become upset and then the only thing that exists in their world is getting their power back. Just like if a parent or teacher accidentally bullies a child and then, instead of cleaning up the conversation and having that child understand that it was a mistake, apologize and say it won't happen again, they let the child go out into the world and look for some way to get their psychological power back. Imagine a child who accidentally, or intentionally, gets bullied by their teacher and then leaves the classroom. Their main focus will be to give another student a mean look, shut someone down or respond negatively to someone so that other person gets upset and they feel better about them self. That is the bully victim circle that we need to try so hard to break. Parents, let's now turn our focus to our children. I invite you to listen as though you were a child in these situations. You never know if the following conversations could help you shift something in your life as well as your children's."

Yensei then addressed the kids directly and said to them, "If you feel like you are a bully and don't know why, my recommendation would be to think about who bullies you, whether it's at home or at school and tell an adult as fast as possible so that the bullying may stop. I've seen situations where a child came up to me after a program and said 'I now know why I bully my friends because of who bullies me at home.' Once they discovered who was bullying that child, and the situation was remedied, that child immediately stopped being a bully." This got Zachary thinking, "I wonder who bullies Billy that has him get so mad that he bullies me. I wish he was here for this program."

Yensei continued, "In our classes, we teach physical self-defense when we are physically attacked. Mental bullying requires mental self-defense. Just like physical self-defense, you may never need to use it, but it is a very good skill to have just in case you need it. The reality is that there are mean people in the world. If you are getting made fun of, today we will learn two effective techniques to walk away powerfully and with your head held up high. A mental bully is looking for a response or a reaction. If you kids show any facial expression, whether sadness, upset, or anger, the bully wins. The only word in the English language that I've found to disarm a verbal attack is "And?" Saying "And?" to any mental attack puts the focus back in the mental bully's lap. The key is to avoid including an attitude in the saying of "And?" so that the bully doesn't get a response.

The second technique to be used with "And?" is what I call the "Power Look". The "Power Look" completely eliminates any and all micro-expressions on the human face, taking away all emotional responses from the face of the person giving the "Power Look." The secret is to look at the top of the forehead of the mental bully and avoid connecting with their eyes. This makes your face go completely blank. Using the "Power Look" in combination with saying "And?" will show the mental bully that there is no reaction to the mental bullying." Yensei turned towards the parents and said, "As with anything in life, this must be practiced with your children repeatedly for them to be successful. Try it yourself in any environment where you have an adult bully."

Yensei faced the children again and asked for a helper. He picked a little girl who was hiding in the back and raised her hand. Her curly red hair and bright red glasses stood out as she slowly walked to the front. "What's your name, young lady?" he asked. "Poppy," she replied quietly. He warmly smiled at her and held his hand out for a high five. She immediately smiled and high fived him with a smack that he wasn't expecting. "Thank you for coming up here to help. Can you help me show all the kids and parents here how easy it is to stand up to a mental bully?" he asked. Poppy nodded her head. "Poppy, have you ever been made fun of?" he inquired. She nodded a woeful yes and looked down at the ground.

"I promise you that if we practice today and you listen to what I tell you, you won't be able to be mentally bullied again." Her gaze rose from the ground directly to his eyes and she beamed with hope. "Now Poppy, when you are ready, I'm going to do what a mental bully does and make fun your hair, clothing, glasses and anything else I can find. Remember that the bully is looking for a response. What word do I want you to say?" She immediately responded "AND!" loudly and passionately. "Exactly!" he exclaimed and high-fived her. "And after you say it three times, then walk away." Yensei proceeded to make fun of her red hair and her glasses. Her first response was an immediate reaction. Yensei told her that she was doing great and to keep trying. "Take a breath if you like. That helps me when someone tries to mentally bully me," he said. "People bully you?" Poppy asked. "They try. I don't allow it. No one can bully you without you letting them. That is called being responsible for your own feelings. It's not easy.

101

That's why we practice. Now, are you OK with showing me how strong you are and practicing again?" She responded even louder "YES!"

This time, Yensei made fun of her clothing and her light up shoes. Poppy looked at his eyes, her face showing emotion, and then it happened. Her face went blank. Every emotion left and she said "And?" Yensei egged her on. "Your red head is ugly." "And?" she said in a strong and firm voice. "Your glasses are silly looking." She said "And?" for the last time, turned around and walked away. The room erupted with applause from the adults. The smile on Poppy's face was that of confidence and pure joy.

"Now it is everyone else's turn. I'm going to bully everyone here and if you react, the bully wins. If you give me the "Power Look" and say 'And?' then you win." Before Yensei had the chance to start, one parent spoke loudly and said "I don't want you to bully my son in the green shirt up front. Joey, raise your hand." No hand came up so the parent repeated themself. "Joey! Raise your hand!" A hand slowly rose that was connected to a timid boy with fear in his eyes. Yensei spoke directly to the parent. "Don't you want your child to practice the tools that they may need to use in the future?" The parent replied, "I don't want him to get upset and then I have to hear it from his mother." Yensei warmly smiled and said, "How upset do you think he's going to be if he becomes a continuous victim of a bully? This program is designed to protect your children. What if he fell out of a boat in a lake? Wouldn't it be a good idea if he had already taken swimming lessons just in case it happens?"

The parent responded "He can't swim. He got scared so we stopped them." Yensei looked at the child sitting there quietly and chose to take a stand for the child even if their own parent wouldn't. "Sir, I'm going to be as honest as possible with you right now because I already know the probable, almost certain future for your boy if something doesn't change immediately. Right now, whether you know it or not, you are choosing your own selfishness over the safety and happiness of your child." The parent snapped back, "How dare you! I absolutely am not!" Yensei continued, "There will be many challenges that your child will face in his life. There will be upset, intimidation and bullying in his future. Especially if he continues to carry himself physically like a victim. If you don't want him to learn these skills, it's because you don't want to feel uncomfortable and have to have a real conversation with him about true life. The problem is that a victim like this will one day turn into a bully and with past situations like the incidents of Columbine, Virginia Tech, and Sandy Hook, your child won't be the only one who may deal with negative repercussions. For this to truly work, we must all try to put aside our selfishness for the betterment of our children and community."

The parent got up furiously, grabbed his son by the arm and stormed off. Other parents started talking to each other about what they just saw. "I ask that you please don't judge him. He doesn't have a choice in how he behaves. You heard him mention that his wife would be upset, so we already know that there is a bully in his life and he is the victim. Until he learns to stand up for himself, his child will suffer the consequences. I ask that if any of your children know his child, maybe they can support him in trying these techniques with him and having him practice away from his father. That is another way a bystander can support the current or future victim of bullying."

"That was a great lesson learned in my opinion. Let's get back to empowering your children." Yensei began by pointing out unique characteristics about the children and one by one, they gave him the "Power Look" and said "And?" He then turned his attention to the parents and started to bully them. After some parents were caught off guard, they straightened out, "Power Looked" and said "And?" to Yensei. "Not as easy as it looks, is it?" he joked. The parents nodded in agreement. Now let's discuss the role that bystanders play in bullying situations.

LIFE SKILLS TOOLBOX

Signs to be aware of if your child is being bullied:

- Lack or loss of appetite

- Frequent crying

- Recurrent complaints of physical symptoms such as stomach aches or headaches with no apparent cause

- Unexplained bruises

- Increased passivity or withdrawal

- Sudden drop in grades, or other learning problems

- Not wanting to go to school

- Significant changes in social life like no one is calling or extending invitations

- Sudden change in the way your student/child talks — calling themself a loser, or a former friend a jerk

How did you feel as the driver of the car with your perfect cup of morning tea or coffee...

1. When you were having a good day?
2. After another driver cut you off?
3. After you blocked the other person from merging in front of you?

How do you feel knowing that you **allowed** the person who cut you off to change your mood and ruin your morning? Now that you know, next time you can choose the same response or choose to be happy and break the bullying circle. You only get to have one of the two previous choices.

How do you feel knowing that the person you blocked from merging is now looking for someone to bully? It could be their spouse, their co-worker, their employee or their child. Now that you know, next time you can choose to create a bully or choose to break the bullying circle by not allowing yourself to be bullied and in turn not bullying others.

The "Power Look" and saying "And?" are highly and immediately effective tools for taking away the bully's power. Practice this with friends first and keep it light-hearted if you are playfully teasing each other. Keep saying, "And?" and when they get frustrated, look at the top of their forehead until they look away, laugh, or any other behavior a human does when they are uncomfortable.

Lastly, the statement, "Right now, whether you know it or not, you are choosing your own selfishness over the safety and happiness of your child," tends to upset some adults. Read that sentence over and over until you are open to looking at a different perspective only for the benefit of your child. If your child wants peanut butter and they are highly allergic, you simply know not to give it to them. No matter how much they whine, yell, scream, manipulate and everything else they learn how to do to have you respond. You'd like them to stop all the behaviors just mentioned and you could choose to just give them the peanut butter but you don't because you powerfully choose what is best for your child over the selfish choice of giving in so the chaos stops.

Now that you know that there is a choice involved, you can choose to be like the parent who ran away with his child and like Harry's mother in Chapter 2, who was more interested in her comfort than teaching Harry life skills, or you can choose to teach your children to be prepared for the real world. The world where, to be successful, one must:

- Learn to stand up for themselves

- Work hard to achieve success and self-worth

- Develop a thick skin and understand that there are those who don't want them to succeed and how to ignore and avoid them

- Learn empathy and compassion for others

- Love themselves unconditionally

- Surround themselves with others who are good people

- Do the right thing for yourself and others no matter what the masses (sheople) say, think or do

Being a hero, parent or teacher means choosing what is best for those who you are a hero for over what is best for you the majority of the time.

(Like a diet and a gym routine, everyone has a cheat day once in a while. Allow yourself a day to occasionally choose to yell and bully and make others feel bad about themselves as an option. Remember that this is optional. Somehow, knowing that it is a justifiable option and giving ourselves that freedom to go back removes the internal pattern that makes us feel like we are being bullied into being good people. Then go back to a clean streak of being a hero and you'll still be doing more good than you were before.)

Chapter 9: Bystanders

"Now let's turn our attention to the majority of students who can truly make an impact in decreasing bullying in your children's environments." Yensei continued as he addressed the parents directly. "As your children progress through school, they are going to be observing and processing a lot of information both inside and outside of the classroom. If your child is lucky enough not to be a victim of a bully, then that is a win for them. However, just like in adulthood, bullies and victims do exist and the bystander can be the one who helps eliminate bullying. A bystander is a person (or persons) who is present at an event without participating in it. They are the most ignored and underused resource in our schools. It is typically about 85% of a school's population and they can become desensitized over time to what is happening right in front of them. We would like to think that our children are strong and stand up for their friends or even strangers because those are traits that we can be proud of. Unfortunately, that is not the case. Children who are bystanders often do not get involved because of three things:

1. Being outted by other peers as a tattletale.

2. Fear of becoming a new victim for the bully.

3. Getting in trouble themselves.

Let's address each situation so that your child can have the opportunity to powerfully stand up for their friend or classmate if the situation arises. Being a tattletale or a snitch as a child or adult is frowned upon in any social environment, whether at school, home, or in the workplace. There is a distinction that we need to clarify which solves this problem quickly and effectively. Bystanders must learn the distinction of "In vs. Out". Yensei turned his attention to the children once again. "Kids, if you are walking down the street with your family and you see two bank robbers jump out of their car and run into the bank, what do you do?" The children yelled out, "Call the police," and "Dial 9-1-1." "Yes!" Yensei said.

He continued, "And because of you, the police show up and the bank robbers get arrested and go to jail. My question to you is...are you tattling on the robbers?" One child raised her hand and Yensei pointed at her and asked, "What do you think?" The girl said "It's not tattling because the robbers are doing something bad." As other children around her nodded, Yensei asked another question. "Is it more important to get the bank robbers in trouble or is it more important to get the people in the bank out of trouble?" Voices from the crowd said in unison "Get the people in the bank out of trouble." Yensei shouted "Correct!

When you are trying to get someone in trouble, like telling on someone, then you are tattling and that isn't showing respect. And if your friend or someone you know in school is getting bullied and you try to get them OUT of trouble, then you are being a hero. Just like you would be a hero if you called the police to help with the bank robbers. Remember that you and the police are a team when you work together to stop the bank robbers. If you didn't call them, they never would have come. Teamwork and being a hero go together like peanut butter and jelly. What other heroes can you find in your school who can help you?"

The children raised their hands and yelled out "Your teacher", "The principal", "The security guard." "Correct again. You kids are so smart!" Yensei exclaimed. "And this brings us to the second reason why bystanders don't get involved."

Yensei made eye contact with the parents again and spoke. "Fear of becoming a new victim for the bully is easily understandable and 100% a legitimate concern if a child is discovered by a bully to be the one who had them get in trouble. If you, as the adult, saw a bank being robbed and you had your cell phone on you, would you call the police in front of the bank robbers so that they could identify you or would you call the police somewhere where the bank robbers couldn't see you? I assume you would make the phone call from a hidden and secure location to protect yourself first and foremost. That would also be the ideal situation if a child sees another child getting bullied and reports it to a teacher. Unfortunately, not every single teacher is trained in specific bullying prevention techniques and might say to the child that they would like them to show them where the bullying is happening.

If the child walks the teacher to the bully, all that will happen is the bully will lie, the current victim will be too afraid to admit they are getting bullied, and the child that was brave enough to stand up for the victim will now become the bully's next victim and will never stand up for another friend again. Instruct the children to say to that teacher 'No. I do not want to be the bully's next victim.' Then go find another adult and tell them where the bullying is happening. This may not be a popular choice with the teacher but it is the best choice to keep a powerful and empathetic child safe so they may help others again. The last reason why bystanders don't like to get involved is that they are afraid of getting in trouble themselves."

Yensei turned his focus to address the children once again. "What does your school tell you to do when someone else is making fun of you?" Yensei asked. One child answered, "Tell a teacher." A second child said to walk away. "That's a good idea. And if you use the "Power Look" and say 'And?', you'll walk away strong and powerful. Now what does your school say you should do when someone is beating you up? And I mean when a physical bully knocks you on the ground and starts hitting you." An eight year old boy said, "Walk away." At least three other children nodded in agreement. "I want to be 100% clear on what you just said. Who told you to walk away when someone is hitting you?" The same eight year old said, "My teacher and my guidance counselor."

He continued, "There was a 5th grader who kept tripping me and pushing me down last year. I told my teacher and then my guidance counselor. They told me that if I put my hands up to stop him or push him back, that I would be suspended and sent home." The eight year old's mother was squirming in her seat and her body language showed that she was completely unaware of anything that her son was saying. "So what did you do?" asked Yensei. "I tried to stay away from him. I would stay in my classes and ask for extra help and I would wait for the hallway to be clear and then go to my next class. What else could I do? I did what my teacher said to do and nothing changed."

"Parents, here lies the problem. We now live in a society where some of what is being taught in your child's school isn't teaching your children about the true rules of society. As an adult, if another adult assaults you and you defend yourself, do you face the same consequences as your attacker? Of course not. The police arrive and do their job by interviewing bystanders and truly getting to the truth of what happened. Then you, as the victim, are asked if you want to press charges against your attacker. That is not the case in your schools. Instead of doing the work and solving the problem, they are teaching your children to keep the victim mentality. What happens if that mentality stays with them when they are off the bus heading home or playing outside at a park on the weekend?

If your children aren't told what your expectations are and they assume, then they will stay a victim much longer." The parents in the room started to grumble amongst themselves. It looked like what Yensei was saying was hitting home with some of them. Yensei saw this response and continued. "What happens when your daughter keeps her victim mentality and her prom date gets too aggressive? Or your son is on a sports team and a player on the other team tries to get under his skin with upsetting comments? How do you want your child to respond and react? Another thing to think about are the consequences on the entire school when a child is continuously bullied, is taught to stay a victim, and one day eventually has an emotional breakdown. He does what most victims do and now becomes the bully, but this time, with an automatic weapon, looking to bully those who bullied him.

This bullying circle can only stop with one thing - communication between you and your children. We are going to take a break now and I invite you to have one of the most important conversations that you will ever have with your child and shift the way their lives will turn out. And parents, please make sure to explain to your children what consequences await them when they get home after dealing with a bullying situation. And by that, I mean that if you tell your child that you approve of them physically defending themselves against a physical attacker, when the school suspends them, there will be no negative consequences for them standing up for themselves."

Yensei took out an easel and wrote down the following:

Four questions I should ask my parents:

1. What do you want me to do if someone is making fun of me in school?

2. What do you want me to do if someone is hitting me in school?

3. What do you want me to do if someone is hitting me outside of school?

4. What do you want me to do if someone is making fun of me on the computer?

The parents and children started talking and Yensei was intrigued, yet not surprised, when he walked around and saw the surprise on the faces of the children. After about 10 minutes, Yensei got everyone's attention back and asked the children what they talked about. One girl, who looked about

10 years old, raised her hand and said, "My mommy told me that if someone hits me in school, I should tell them to stop and tell a teacher. And if it doesn't stop, I can block and hit her back!" She then looked to her mother and her mother smiled at her and gave her a thumbs up. The joy and hope beaming from the little girl's eyes said everything. She'd just learned that she didn't have to be a victim anymore. One by one, children raised their hands and talked about how their parents didn't want them to start fights but it was OK for them to finish them.

"I'm glad that you had this opportunity to discuss your expectations with your children." Yensei said to the parents. "My recommendation to reinforce strength in your child and to ensure that they are never a victim of bullying again is to create a constant reminder of the day they stood up for themself. We teach your children self-defense. They use it on a physical bully. The bully stops picking on them and the rest of the school hears what happened and your child is never picked on again. When they get suspended, take a day off from work. Take them out for pizza, ice cream and a movie. Spend $20 on a trophy that they can display proudly. Congratulate them for standing up for themself or the friend they defended. Make a note of that date and celebrate it every year to remind them of the strength and power that they have inside. I sincerely thank you for coming out today to this workshop and if you have any questions about enrolling your child in self-defense classes, please see me after. I hope you have a wonderful and powerful day. Namastahyah!"

LIFE SKILLS TOOLBOX

If you feel that you would prefer that your child choose not to get involved in other people's business, including helping out another child, then that is 100% your choice and your prerogative if that's the way that you want to live. I invite you to look back into your own life and see if there was a time where you stood up for someone else and it led to a negative consequence for you and/or someone you cared about. That would then explain why you don't want the same thing to happen to your child. You can choose to give that up or not. If you want your child to be empathetic to others and be a true leader and good person, then address each point made in the chapter by teaching your child/student:

1. The difference between being a tattletale and being a hero with the "In vs. Out" conversation

2. How to avoid becoming a bully's next victim by bravely reinforcing that they do not, under any circumstances, let the bully know that they reported the bullying situation

3. Discuss the four questions with them, if you are a parent, and let them know that they will not get in trouble at home for standing up for their friend and the opposite will happen as you celebrate their bravery and kindness for others.

Chapter 10: What Can You/I Do to Help?

It was a warm early Saturday morning and Olivia was sitting in her favorite pink rocking chair with her eyes glued to a popular kids program on the television in the living room. Julia peeked in on her before she began preparing breakfast. It had been a few weeks since Zachary told his mother about the bullying on the bus and he hadn't said anything about it to her since. Julia had become extremely busy with a new responsibility at her own school and had stopped asking Zachary about it. "If he's still getting picked on, I'm sure he would have told me," she thought to herself.

Zachary slinked out of his bedroom and down the stairs heading towards the living room. He passed by the kitchen and didn't respond when Julia said,

"Good morning." As he walked into the living room, his eyes fell on his sister and particularly the smile on her face from enjoying her show. As she giggled, he grunted. She laughed louder and he got madder. Zachary couldn't stand that he still felt afraid and powerless and she was enjoying herself. He went to grab the remote control to change the channel. Olivia caught him going for it out of the corner of her eye and grabbed it first. Zachary snapped and pushed Olivia.

Olivia ran over to her mother and sobbed to her what happened. Julia barreled to the living room to find Zachary sitting and watching television like nothing happened. When she asked him what happened and why he did it, he simply shrugged his shoulders and said, "I don't know." After repeating herself two more times without success, she sent

Zachary to his room after breakfast. Zachary finished eating quickly and ran up to his room and slammed the door. Julia didn't know what was going on with him and then the phone rang and she forgot what she was thinking about.

As his door slammed, he started to cry. He ran to his bed and grabbed his pillow with both of his hands and screamed into it. He screamed and cried and screamed some more. A movie ran in his mind of Billy pushing him on the bus. He saw Billy punching him in the eye two days ago. He saw himself looking out the window of the bus in fear as the bus approached Billy's stop. Zachary wanted it to stop. He wanted to hit Billy back with every muscle in his body. He wanted to, but he didn't.

Each morning and each afternoon Zachary knew he would see Billy and each morning and each afternoon he knew that he had to choose not to block or hit back. As his eyes filled with tears, he repeatedly asked himself, "Why is this happening? Why won't anyone stop it?" He stared out the bedroom window with rage and sadness filling every inch of his body. Zachary watched a bird fly past his window chirping with glee. The bird seemed so happy flying around. There was no fear in the flying. There was no sadness in the flying. There was only peace in the flying.

Julia came down the steps to see her husband and daughter waiting for them to head out. Julia checked the back door one more time before heading towards the main entrance. She walked through the living room and glanced at the pictures of her beautiful family as she took Olivia's hand in a gentle yet firm manner and walked with her to the car. The drive would be about 30 minutes and Olivia was getting fidgety in her car seat. "We'll be there soon." Dad said to her as they made eye contact in the rear view mirror. As they arrived Olivia got excited to see her Pop-Pop and Na-Na walking towards the car. Dad let Olivia out as Julia walked towards her parents. She had been strong on the car ride there but seeing her parents had reality settle in hard and she dropped to her knees sobbing. Her mother and father immediately embraced her and said "Honey, we know this is so hard for you. I know you know he is with the angels now and he misses you tremendously. Just as much as you miss him."

Olivia didn't really understand what had happened to her brother. Her mommy told her that Zachary fell and went to be with the angels. Olivia looked around at all the people that had come to say goodbye to her brother. She recognized Lucy and her mom. She remembered what happened at their birthday party and how she stood up for her. She remembered Harry and his mother from the Yogarate® school and how upset they both were when they didn't get their way. Yensei was standing behind them amongst many others from the dojo. Olivia heard someone called Mr. Phillips was standing across from them with his head down crying. She didn't know who the older boy was or the two people behind him were but they didn't look too happy. She tried to read the letters on his jacket. "B...I...L...L...Y. Billy," she shouted out loud excitedly and pointed to his shirt. He immediately looked at her turned and ran away with his parents chasing after him.

"This is my fault," was a thought that floated through the minds of some of the attendees as they stood with Billy's family looking at the casket. "What could I have done differently? Did I do everything I could? Did I do what was right? What can I do in the future?"

LIFE SKILLS TOOLBOX

I invite you to consider this as a wakeup call. This is reality and does happen. Below are solutions and actions that each and every person in a child's life can take. Now, you get to choose to be selfish or to be their champion. Only you and the person in the mirror everyday will know your choice.

Actions you can take if you are a:

Parent, in general:

- Instruct your child to ask you the four questions and respond honestly and clearly.
- If you personally are mentally bullied, use the "Power Look" and repeat "And?" after every

comment. Three times, at the most, and then walk away powerfully and proudly.

- If you accidentally bully your child, have a clean-up conversation with them so they don't feel the need to bully someone else.

Parent of Victim:

- Teach your child the "Power Look" and why to say "And?"

- Keep watch of their eating habits and any changes in behavior, including them becoming new bullies themselves.

- Talk to your child about giving them permission to defend themself only if they are getting physically bullied. Once they have that, the next time the bully attacks them, block to the best of their ability and then squeeze their hand hard and hammerfist the bully right on the nose.

- Go through the school's proper procedures to alert them of bullying situations. If you haven't heard from the school first, alert the teacher, anti-bullying specialist, principal, district anti-bullying coordinator, or guidance counselor. Research your district's anti-bullying policies and procedures online so you know what to expect and how quickly actions will be taken.

- On the day they are suspended for defending themself, celebrate and let the world know. If their school is not handling a bullying situation and ignoring you, immediately get an attorney to write a letter so the school takes action. The first parent with an attorney's letter usually gets the school to respond in their favor...

<u>Parent of Bully</u>: PLEASE DON'T SIMPLY SAY "THIS ISN'T ME" AND SKIP OVER THIS SECTION. YOUR CHILD'S FUTURE MAY DEPEND ON YOUR ABILITY TO BE HUMBLE AND TAKE RESPONSIBILITY FOR YOUR, AND THEIR, ACTIONS.

- Look inside and ask yourself, first, if your child is a bully in response to the way you treat them, intentionally or accidentally. If you just realized that you bully them, then forgive yourself for you knew not what you did and now it *is* your responsibility to choose to continue or stop.

- Look at your own life and see who bullies you and who you have been giving your power to.

- Take actions to eliminate the bullies in your life and set the example for your children.

<u>Parent of Bystander</u>:

- Teach your child the concept of "In vs. Out". If they see someone getting bullied, first ask whether they are trying to get the bully in trouble or the victim out of trouble.

- Instruct them to go find an adult to let them know where the bullying is happening and make sure they don't go with the adult to investigate. If no adults are around, go find more friends to help the victim.

- When asking the four questions, answer them also with your expectations for them regarding standing up for their friends or fellow students.

<u>All school employees including teachers, counselors, principals and administrators</u>:

Try and remember who inspired you or why you chose to take on the path of being an educator or administrator. At some point in your life, your commitment to truly making a difference and empowering children to become amazing adults had you choose your career path. We all know it wasn't for the paycheck! Put yourself in the small shoes of a victim who doesn't want to go to school and cries themselves to sleep because they aren't being helped. Were you ever bullied or know someone who was? Think of the parents that have to watch their child be terrified while they feel powerless to help.

They hope, trust and believe that **YOU** will do your best to take care of the physical, emotional, and mental well-being of their most precious gifts. If you are failing these innocent children and the parents, now **YOU** get to make a choice. **YOU** get to choose between the imaginary fears that you create in your mind about losing your job because of the imaginary lawsuit that some bully's parents bully you with, making you their victim. OR **YOU** can choose to be a POWERFUL and UNSTOPPABLE force and be a CHAMPION for them. You can choose to remember why you became an educator. You get to choose to be done with feeling like a victim of the person above you and stop being a bystander while children you are responsible for are being bullied. **YOU CAN CHOOSE TO DO WHAT IS RIGHT!**

Teacher:

- Be aware of potential bullying situations arising by reading body language.

- Be a responsible adult and, if you accidentally create a bully, have a clean-up conversation to ensure that the child doesn't leave your presence looking to bully others.
- Have conversations with your classroom regarding the information learned before to teach:
    - Bullies - how to figure out who bullies them to stop the bullying circle
    - Victims - the "Power Look" and to say "And?" when being mentally bullied
    - Bystanders - that letting you know of a bullying situation happening is not tattling

<u>Guidance Counselor/Anti-Bullying Specialist</u>:

- Think about your position as the Anti-Bullying Specialist. Did you request this position or were you bullied into taking on this role? If you don't 100% choose this role, there may be a hint of being a victim of the situation in the back of your mind which may interfere with you handling bullying situations to the best of your ability.

- Keep the victim and bully apart initially. Don't try to bring them together to mediate and work it out together first. Would you like to be in the same room, at the same table, as a stalker or attacker to "work things out?" Let's be real. Adults don't need to "work things out" and "learn to get along" in life when someone harasses them. The harasser is required to simply stay away from that person. Not all kids NEED to get along. Teach your students reality instead of some pie-eyed false reality.

School Principal & Superintendent: (The following information was from an elementary school principal who works in the South Brunswick District in New Jersey that has significantly lower bullying incidents than many of the neighboring districts due to their effective approaches and the systems they have in place.)

- At the beginning of the school year, have an assembly and discuss expectations for the students. Revisit the code of conduct and Harassment, Intimidation and Bullying (HIB) rules, laws and consequences. Splitting up the age groups K-1, 2-3 and grades 4-5 makes for increased information retention and less miscommunication later on.

- Have lessons on empathy and conflict resolution three times a year from the guidance counselor and Anti-Bullying Specialist in classrooms.

- Give children the words to speak up and the importance of being specific with their words so that every situation doesn't get lumped in as an HIB violation.

- Communicate with children and parents immediately if a situation occurs. Be honest and a good person who chooses to be the victim's champion instead of caving to empty-threatened lawsuits from the bully's parents. Do whatever you can do with your power to protect all the children in your school. Your parents, teachers, and children look to you for support, safety and solutions. Be their champion. Be their hero. Save the next Zachary. You are their hope. Yes, you.

How to Leave a Review!

We need your feedback to help with our non-stop efforts to provide you with the best information possible. Please take a few minutes to leave an honest review of this book by following these easy steps:

1. Go to http://www.amazon.com

2. Search for the book you wish to review by typing the title of this book in the search box at the top of the page.

3. Click on the image of this book on the search results page.

4. Just below the book title and author's name, there is a link to the reviews that have already been left, if any, or the link to leave a review. Click on the link.

5. At the top of the page that opens, click on the "Create Your Own Review" button.

6. Follow the prompts to leave your own review of the book.

Thank you!

About the Author

Ron Shuali, M.Ed has spent over 15 years working and presenting in the education marketplace. He is an author, top motivational speaker and presenter with  expertise in the preschool and elementary school arena. Ron has spoken at continuing professional development national and regional conferences for organizations like the NAEYC, NJEA and the Goddard Systems just to name a few and presents school assemblies nationally as well.

Ron has been a student of many disciplines of martial arts starting at age 12. His journey began with 5 years of Tae Kwon Do until he attended college. He joined the martial arts club and traveled to other schools to compete in full contact team tournaments. While attending college, he met his second teacher and began studying Wu Shu Kung Fu. After graduating with a Bachelor's from Rutgers University, he met his third teacher and earned his Black Belt in American Freestyle Karate. After 4 years he found his fourth martial arts teacher and began his training on the more internal martial art of Hung Gar Kung Fu. His thirst for continuous knowledge led him to his last teacher as he studied Isshinryu Karate. Currently Ron and his team teach two systems that he developed in dozens of preschools. Shua Fun Do is the art of breathing and fun and Yogarate® which combines yoga and martial art principles which lead to students who embrace deep breathing and self-defense as one.

His vast knowledge of the inner working of the mind led to the creation of some of the most revolutionary and forward thinking award winning programs in existence today. Participants and organizations alike have agreed that his thought-provoking information combined with his comical entertainment background always left the crowd wanting more. "Nobody watches the clock when Ron is on stage."

Through his travels Ron has done everything from stand-up comedy, improvisational theater, teaching in preschools and professional wrestling. This journey taught him the truth about connecting with an audience, from preschooler to professional. His ability to quickly grab the audience with true life stories while simultaneously introducing techniques and concepts is exceptionally effective. The audiences receive the gift of learning through laughter to ensure that they will always walk away thinking and excited to test out the new techniques that were just learned.

48728417R00092

Made in the USA
Middletown, DE
26 September 2017